The Motown Story

In the 1960s, the "Motown Sound" was a dominant force in music, forming the soundtrack for a full generation. Rarely before had one label and one record producer (Berry Gordy) had such a major impact on the music scene. While many African-Americans had felt shut out or overshadowed in rock and roll (despite the prominence of Little Richard and Chuck Berry), Motown was a music that they could call their own, dance to, and sing along with, whether it was Diana Ross and the Supremes, "Little" Stevie Wonder, Marvin Gaye, Smoky Robinson or the Jackson Five. And while nearly all of the Motown stars were African-Americans, the music had such a universal appeal that its songs topped all of the pop charts on a regular basis.

Where did the Motown sound come from? During the 1935-46 period, swing was the thing and most of American popular music came from that style of jazz. However with the end of the big band era, the popular music world split into several different areas. Some musicians played in New Orleans jazz/Dixieland bands, explored bebop, recorded easy-listening projects or became the backup groups for pop singers. Another alternative was offered by early rhythm and blues which came directly from swing. Illinois Jacquet, on Lionel Hampton's 1942 recording of "Flying Home," ushered in an era of honking tenor-saxophonists with his stirring and much-copied solo. Within a few years, many other saxophonists played in a similar exhibitionistic manner, honking, roaring and screaming on their instruments over simple chord structures to excited audiences.

By the mid-1950s, with the saxophone de-emphasized in favor of the guitar, a safer version of dance music that featured vocals aimed at teenagers emerged. It was called rock and roll and was influenced by rhythm & blues, swing, blues, country music and a vocal style that was itself influenced by early black vocal groups, doo wop. While African-Americans had founded many of these styles, the biggest moneymakers in rock and roll were whites.

Berry Gordy aimed to change much of that. Born in Detroit in 1929, Gordy loved both music and boxing. After dropping out of high school, he boxed as a lightweight but soon realized that music was a much more glamorous and potentially lucrative career. He was a talented songwriter and showed a lot of potential from the start. After a stint in the army, he opened a record shop in Detroit. After the store failed, he supported his family by working in an auto plant while writing songs at night. He had his first successes writing for Jackie Wilson starting with 1956's "Reet Petite" which was a hit. He also wrote "Lonely Teardrops," "To Be Loved" and "I'll Be Satisfied" for Wilson and "All I Could Do Was Cry" for Etta James. But while other up-and-coming performers were now coming to Gordy for new material, he realized that he was making very little money from their recordings. He decided that he had to go out on his own and become a businessman.

Berry Gordy set up his own publishing company and, after meeting the young vocalist Smokey Robinson, he became his manager. He co-wrote "Got A Job" which became a hit for Smokey Robinson and the Miracles. Gordy bought a house which he turned into a recording studio, naming it "Hitsville USA." With a loan of $800 from his family, he started two labels, Tamila and Motown, in 1959, merging them together as Motown the following year. His composition "Money (That's What I Want)," which was recorded by Robinson (Motown's vice president), became Motown's first hit. "Way Over There" and "Shop Around" soon followed with "Shop Around" (on which Gordy played piano) becoming the label's first million-selling record. In 1960 the Marvelettes' "Please Mr. Postman" became Motown's first #1 pop hit in the US. It would not be their last. Life began to accelerate.

During 1961-71, Motown released 110 singles that were top 10 hits, a remarkable number for one label. A masterful talent scout who was also brilliant at nurturing new talent, Berry Gordy released music by such major acts as Diana Ross & The Supremes, The Four Tops, The Jackson 5, Stevie Wonder (who Gordy signed when he was just 11), Marvin Gaye, the Temptations, Martha and the Vandellas, Gladys Knight & The Pips, The Spinners, Jr. Walker, The Contours, The Velvelettes, The Spinners, and The Monitors among others. By the mid-1960s, Motown's slogan "The Sound Of Young America' had become very accurate.

What was it about the music of Motown that made it so popular, not only among African Americans but everywhere? The typical Motown record was a mixture of soul music and pop. Its vocal stars not only had beautiful and soulful voices, but they knew how to build up their choruses emotionally to very passionate heights, influenced by gospel music while dealing with universal and secular topics.

The rhythms were infectious, the melodies were catchy, and the lyrics were memorable. While the music was simple enough to be sung by most listeners, it was also sophisticated on many levels. The songs were very original, not based on earlier tunes. The recordings were advanced for the period, utilizing overdubbing, background vocals that emphasized call and response, horn sections and occasional strings. Motown's house band, The Funk Brothers, consisted of brilliant and versatile musicians who could uplift any song. And everything recorded for Motown was danceable.

The 1960s were the era when a segregated American society finally began to become integrated. Motown brought the music of African-Americans into the homes of White Americans. While some earlier black stars broke the color barrier in this way (including Louis Armstrong, Duke Ellington, Count Basie, Nat King Cole, Ella Fitzgerald, Billy Eckstine and Erroll Garner), the entire Motown catalog found its way into the mainstream of American culture, influencing its direction for the next few decades.

Motown was more than just a record company, At Hitsville USA, the recording studio was always open. The building also housed a rehearsal hall, the company's music publishing, promotion department, and booking agency. Artist development classes taught by Maxine Powell gave performers lessons in dealing with the media and the public along with etiquette. Many of the young artists came from poor and working class families in Detroit. They were told that they were setting an example for the African-American artists of future generations. They were taught how to act, dress, and dance on stage (with their acts being largely choreographed) like glamorous and classy stars.

The hits kept coming throughout the 1960s, many written by the team of Brian Holland, Lamont Dozier and Eddie Holland. Among the Motown songs that made it to #1 on the pop charts were Stevie Wonder's "Fingertips," Mary Wells' "My Guy," The Temptations' "My Girl" and "I Can't Get Next To You," The Four Tops' "I Can't Help Myself" and "Reach Out I'll Be There," Marvin Gaye's "I Heard It Through The Grapevine," and quite a few by the Diana Ross and the Supremes including "Where Did Our Love Go," "Baby Love," "Come See About Me," "Stop! In The Name Of Love," "Back In My Arms Again," "I Hear A Symphony," You Can't Hurry Love," "You Keep Me Hangin' On," "Love Is Here And Now You're Gone,' "The Happening," "Love Child" and "Someday We'll Be Together."

In 1966, 22 Motown singles made it to the Top 20 of the pop charts and 75% of all Motown releases landed in the top 100. 1970 found the Jackson 5 having four giant hits with "I Want You Back," "ABC," "The Love You Save," and "I'll Be There." That year Motown also had hits with Smokey Robinson's "The Tears Of A Clown," Edwin Starr's "War" and Diana Ross' "Ain't No Mountain High Enough."

Although it had lasted a long time for the music industry, Motown's success eventually did slow down. In 1970 Diana Ross and the Supremes broke up, with Ross launching a solo career. While Ross, Marvin Gaye, Stevie Wonder, the Jackson 5 and Michael Jackson all were very successful, Motown's dominance in the music business began to lessen. An end of an era was reached in 1972 when Motown relocated to Los Angeles. Berry Gordy and Motown became more involved in films, producing several major movies including Lady Sings The Blues, Mahogany and The Wiz.

Motown was still important in music, not only for repackaging its earlier hits but for its 1970s recordings of Lionel Richie and the Commodores, Rick James, and Teena Marie in addition to Diana Ross, Marvin Gaye, Smokey Robinson and Stevie Wonder. But it was no longer a hit-making machine. By the mid-1980s, Berry Gordy was actually losing money in the company. In June 1988 the 59-year old composer-producer-executive sold Motown (which he had started with $800) for $61 million.

While Motown, which has been bought and sold a few times since then, had had some further hits by Boyz II Men, Johnny Gill, Brian McKnight, Erykah Badu and India Arie in the 1990s and into the 21st century, it has long since become chiefly known for its earlier days. Motown will be forever famous as the legendary label associated with 1960s soul music that introduced a remarkable number of famous songs and talented performers.

Scott Yanow, *author of 11 books including The Great Jazz Guitarists, The Jazz Singers, Jazz On Film and Jazz On Record 1917-76*

4

Music Minus One
50 Executive Boulevard · Elmsford, New York 10523-1325
800-669-7464 (US) · 914-592-1188 (International) · e-mail: info@musicminusone.com
www.musicminusone.com

MMO 3936

Music Minus One Trombone

Motown Trombone

CONTENTS

Complete Track	Minus Track			Page
	11	Tuning Notes	(0:29)	
1	12	What's Going On	(3:22)	6
2	13	Got To Give It Up	(3:17)	10
3	14	I'll Be Doggone	(2:53)	14
4	15	Ain't That Peculiar	(3:08)	18
5	16	Mercy Mercy Me (The Ecology)	(2:45)	23
6	17	Pride and Joy	(2:15)	27
7	18	That's The Way Love Is	(2:46)	30
8	19	How Sweet It Is To Be Loved By You	(3:05)	34
9	20	(Love Is Like A) Heat Wave	(2:44)	38
10	21	The Way You Do The Things You Do	(2:43)	42

MMO 3936

What's Going On

Words and Music by
Marvin Gaye, Al Cleveland and Renaldo Benson

2222

Got To Give It Up

Words and Music by
Marvin Gaye

12

par - ty_____ all night long._____ Let me slip in - to_____

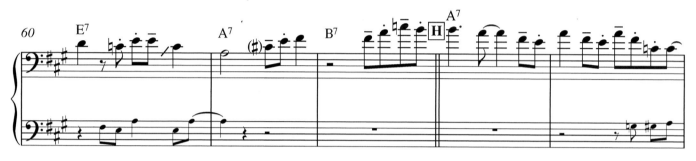

your e - rot - ic zone._____ Move it up,

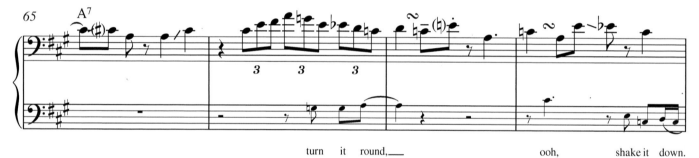

turn it round,_____ ooh, shake it down.

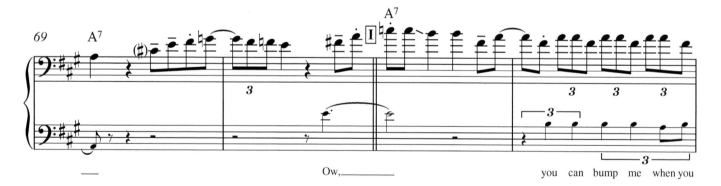

_____ Ow,_____ you can bump me when you

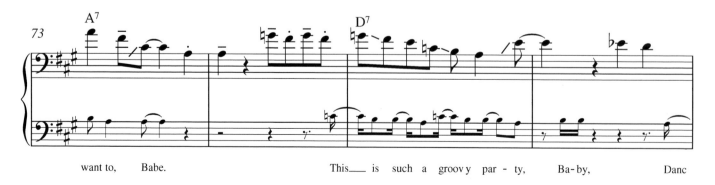

want to, Babe. This___ is such a groovy par - ty, Ba-by, Danc

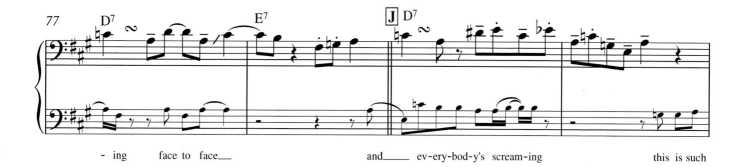

- ing   face to face___   and___ ev-ery-bod-y's scream-ing   this is such

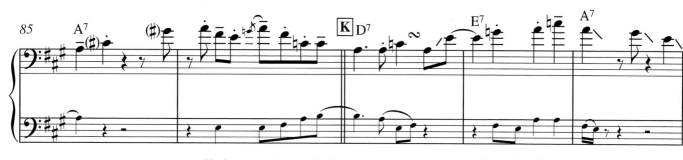

a groov-y place._   Whoo,   all___ the young la - dies   are so   fine.

__   You're   mov-ing your bod - y___   leaves me with no   doubt;

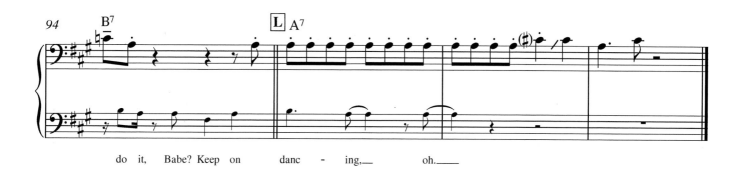

Know what you're think - ing,Ba - by,   you want to turn me   out.___   Think I'm gon-na let you

do it, Babe? Keep on   danc - ing,___ oh.___

13

MMO 3936

I'll Be Doggone

Words and Music by
Pete Moore and Marv Tarplin

Well, eve-ry wom-an should try to be____ what-ev-er her man___ wants her___ to be,____ and I don't

____ want much, all I want from you___ is for you to be true to me.____ I'd be dog-gone if

love ain't a man's best friend, oh,___ and I'll be dog-gone___ if you___ ain't the lov-ing end.

____ Though I know___ you make me feel___ like no-bod-y could. If I

ev-er found out that you're no___ good, then I would-n't be dog-gone,____ I'd be long gone.

Well,__ I would-n't be dog - gone,_____ I'd be long gone.____ I_____

would - n't be dog - gone, goin' catch me a train._____

No__ Ba - by, I would-n't be...

Ain't That Peculiar

Words and Music by
Eddie Holland and Norman Whitfield

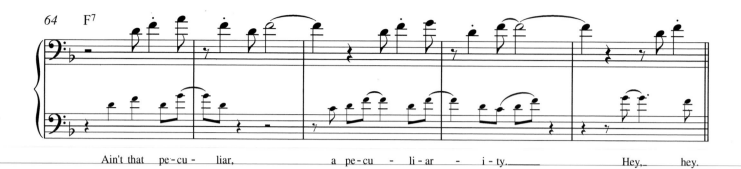

Ain't that pe-cu - liar, a pe-cu - li-ar - i -ty.___ Hey,_ hey.

Ah, ah, ah,___ hey, hey,

___ ah, ah, ah,___ hey,_ hey,___ ah, ah, ah,

___ ah, ah, ah.___ Ooh,___ I've cried so much,___just like_ a child

___ thats_ lost a toy.___ May-be, Ba - by, you think___ these tears_ I cry___ are tears_ of joy.

A child can cry so much__ un - til__ you do e - very-thing they say,_____ but un -

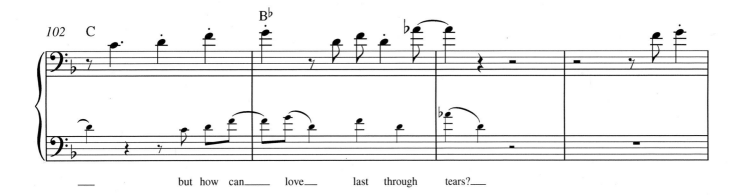

like a child my tears__don't help__ me to get my way.__ I know love can last through years,

but how can__ love__ last through tears?__

Uh, ain't that pe - cu - liar, Ba - by, pe - cu - li - ar - i - ty._____

Ain't it pe-cu - liar, Ho - ney, what you__ are ask - ing me?__ Said I don't un-der-stand

__ it,__ Ba - by. It's so strange some - times.__ Ain't it pe-cu - liar,__ Dar - lin'.

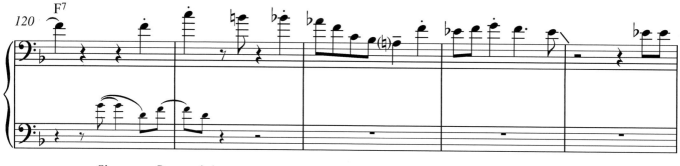

Oh,__ Ba - by!

Mercy Mercy Me

Words and Music by
Marvin Gaye

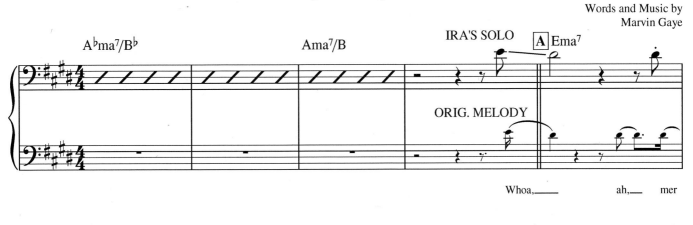

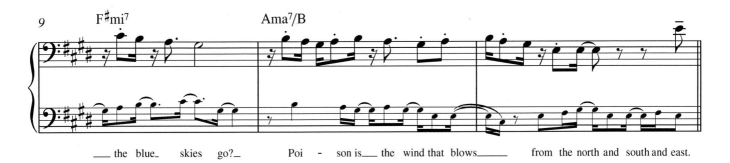

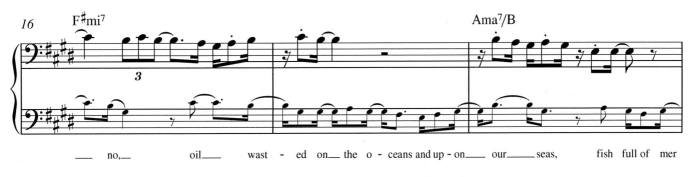

- cu - ry.___ Ah,_____ oh,___ mer - cy mer - cy me,_____ ah,___ things

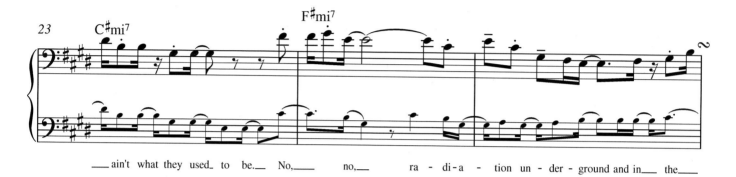

___ain't what they used_ to be.__ No,___ no,___ ra - di - a - tion un - der - ground and in__ the___

___ sky;_ An - i - mals and birds___who live_near by_ are___ dy - ing. Oh,___ mer

- cy mer - cy me,_____ ah,___ things___ain't what they used_____

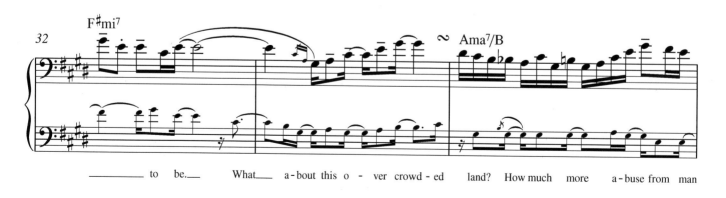

_____ to be.__ What___ a - bout this o - ver crowd - ed land? How much more a - buse from man

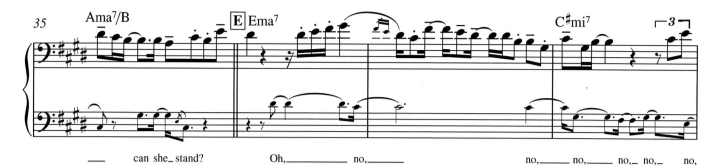

can she_ stand?   Oh,_____ no,_____   no,____ no,____ no,_ no,_ no,

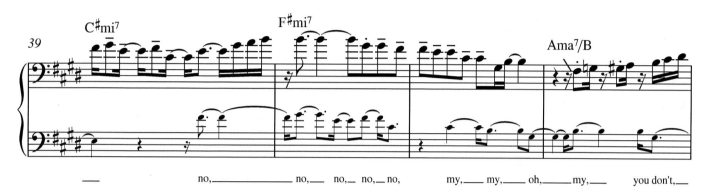

___ no,_____ no,__ no,_ no,_no,   my,___ my,____ oh,____ my,___ you don't,___

___   ooh._____

Pride and Joy

Words and Music by
Norman Whitfield, Marvin Gaye and William Stevenson

28

MMO 3936

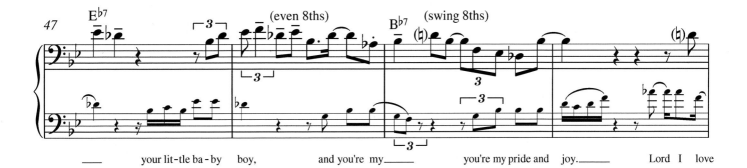

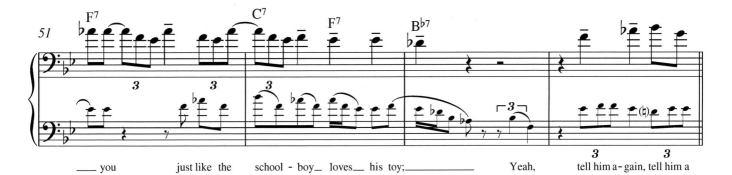

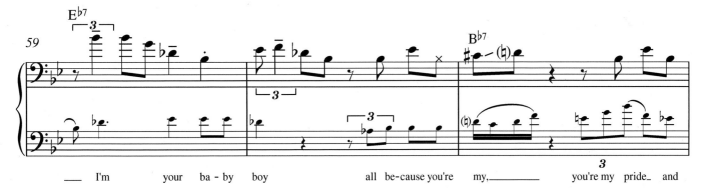

That's the Way Love Is

Words and Music by
Norman Whitfield and Barrett Strong

Oh,_____ that's the way_____ love is, Ba - by.

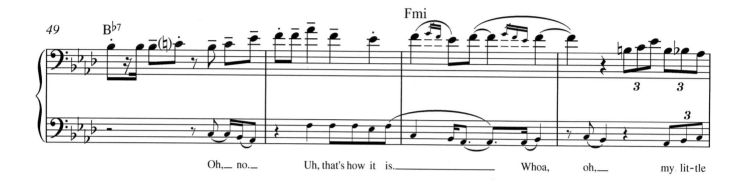

Oh,__ no.__ Uh, that's how it is._____ Whoa, oh,__ my lit-tle

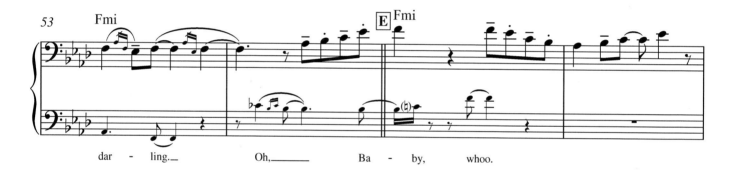

dar - ling.__ Oh,_____ Ba - by, whoo.

Oh,__ lis-ten to____me lit-tle dar-ling; The road of love__ gets rough some - times, don't

let it get the best of___ you.___ Said I've been hurt by___ love___ so___ man-y times so I

know just what you're go-ing through. Ah,___ you wish that you were ne-ver___ born.___ You bet-ter for

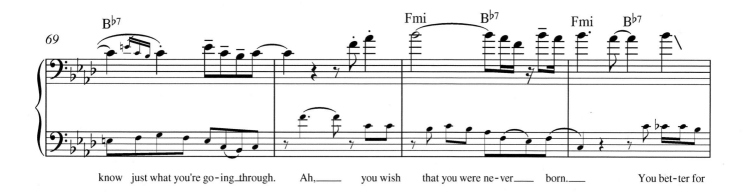

get him now that he's gone;___ Just re - mem - ber, that's the way___

love is___ Ba - by. Ooh,___ oh,___ that's the way.___

How Sweet It Is
(To Be Loved By You)

Words and Music by
Brian Holland, Lamont Dozier and Eddie Holland

How sweet it is___ to be loved by you.___ Yes Ba - by, ooh,_____

___ how sweet it is___ to be___ loved by you.___ Ohh, Ba - by,

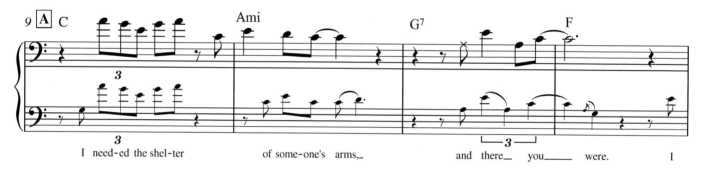

I need-ed the shel-ter of some-one's arms,_ and there_ you___ were. I

need - ed some - one to un-der-stand my ups and_ downs,_ and there_ you___ were,

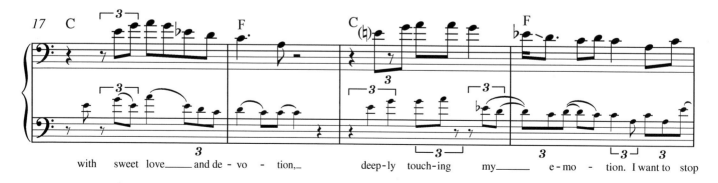

with sweet love___ and de - vo - tion,_ deep-ly touch-ing my___ e - mo - tion. I want to stop

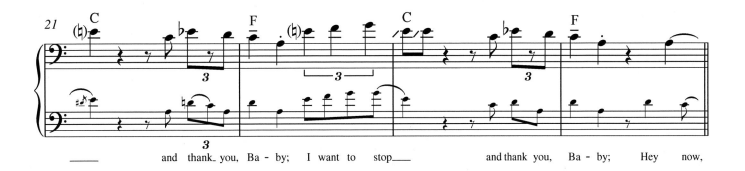

and thank_ you, Ba - by; I want to stop___ and thank you,_ Ba - by; Hey now,

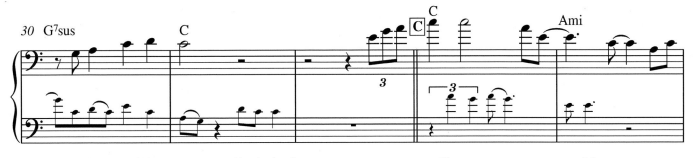

__ how sweet it is___ to be loved by you._ Oh Ba - by,_____ how sweet it is_

__ to be loved by you._ Yes it is. Close my eyes_ at night,

and won-der what would I be with - out you_ in my_ life._ Eve - ry-thing was just a___ bore;

all the things I did,___ seems I've done 'em be-fore, but you bright-en up for_____ my_ days

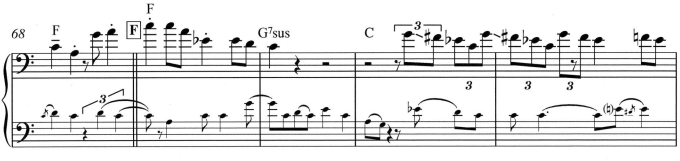

Ba- by; Oh,_____ how sweet it is_____ to be___loved by you.__ Tell____ the truth Ba - by,____

how sweet it is_____ to be___ loved by you.__ Well it's like su - gar_____ for my soul,____

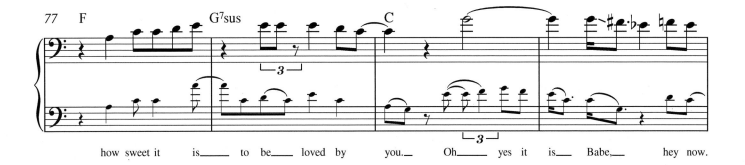

how sweet it is_____ to be___ loved by you.__ Oh____ yes it is____ Babe,____ hey now.

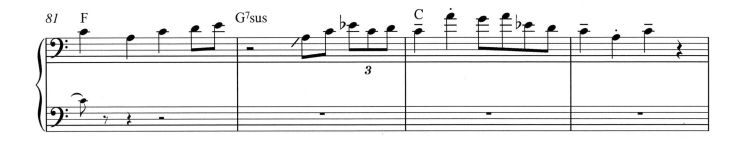

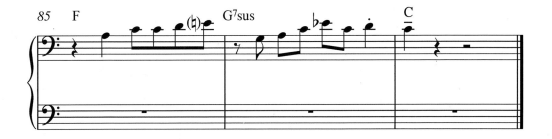

38

Heat Wave

Words and Music by
Edward Holland, Lamont Dozier and Brian Holland

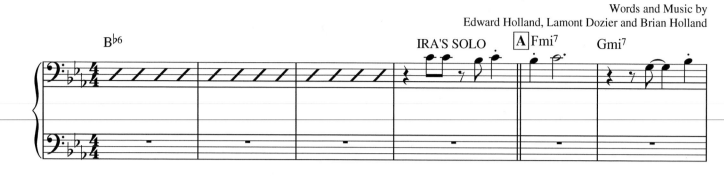

When-ev - er I'm with him___ some-thing in - side___ still

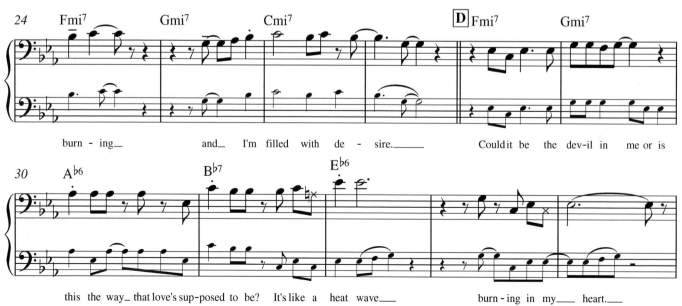

burn - ing___ and_ I'm filled with de - sire.___ Could it be the dev-il in me or is

this the way_ that love's sup-posed to be? It's like a heat wave___ burn-ing in my___ heart.___

88

40

The Way You Do The Things You Do

Words and Music by
Smokey Robinson and Bobby Rogers

you know you could have been a flow - er.___ If good looks was a min - ute,

you know that you could be an hour.___ The way you stole my heart,___

you know you could have been a cool crook. And, Ba - by, you're so smart,

you know you could have been a school-book. Well,___ you could have been an - y - thing that you

want-ed to,___ and I can tell___ the way you do the things you do. Ah, Ba

- by, yeah.___

44

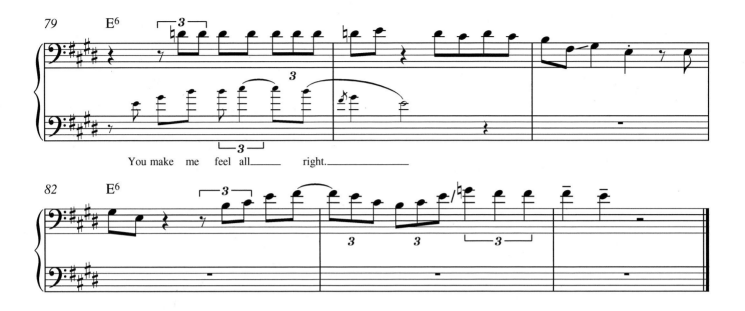

You make me feel all_____ right._____

A WORLD OF TROMBONE MUSIC FROM MUSIC MINUS ONE
Quality Accompaniment Editions since 1950
www.musicminusone.com

CHAMBER CLASSICS
MMO CD 3904	Baroque Brass and Beyond: Quintets
MMO CD 3909	Classical Trombone Solos
MMO CD 3905	Music for Brass Ensemble
MMO CD 3927	Sticks & Bones: Brass Quintets
MMO CD 3908	STRAVINSKY L'Histoire du Soldat

INSPIRATIONAL CLASSICS
MMO CDG 1203	Christmas Memories

INSTRUMENTAL CLASSICS WITH ORCHESTRA
MMO CD 3930	Band Aids: Concert Band Favorites
MMO CD 3929	Popular Concert Favorites w/Orch

JAZZ, STANDARDS AND BIG BAND
MMO CD 2044	2+2=5: A Study Odd Times
MMO CD 3974	Bacharach Revisited
MMO CD 3985	Back to Basics in the Style of the Basie Band
MMO CD 3907	Big Band Ballads: Tenor or Bass Trombone
MMO CD 3926	From Dixie to Swing
MMO CD 3933	Isle of Orleans
MMO CD 3910	Jazz Standards w/Strings
MMO CD 3934	New Orleans Classics
MMO CD 2004	Northern Lights
MMO CD 3975	PCH Pacific Coast Horns, vol. 1: Longhorn Serenade
MMO CD 3976	PCH Pacific Coast Horns, vol. 2: 76 Trombones and other favs (Int-Adv)
MMO CD 3977	PCH Pacific Coast Horns, vol. 3: Where Trombone Reigns (Int-Adv)
MMO CD 3972	Play Ballads w/a Band
MMO CD 3935	Standards for Trombone (Ira Lepus, trombone)
MMO CD 2024	Studio City
MMO CD 3973	Swing with a Band
MMO CD 2014	Take One (minus Lead Trombone)
MMO CD 3921	Chicago-Style Jam Session
MMO CD 3923	Adventures in N.Y. & Chicago Jazz
MMO CD 3906	Unsung Hero: Great Sinatra Standards

LAUREATE MASTER SERIES CONCERT SOLOS
MMO CD 3911	Beginning Solos, v. I (Brevig)
MMO CD 3912	Beginning Solos, v. II (Friedman)
MMO CD 3913	Int. Solos, v. I (Brown)
MMO CD 3914	Int. Solos, v. II (Friedman)
MMO CD 3915	Advanced Solos, v. I (Brown)
MMO CD 3916	Advanced Solos, v. II (Brevig)
MMO CD 3917	Advanced Solos, v. III (Brown)
MMO CD 3918	Advanced Solos, v. IV (Friedman)
MMO CD 3919	Advanced Solos, v. V (Brevig)

STUDENT SERIES
MMO CD 3932	Classic Themes: 27 Easy Songs
MMO CD 3903	Easy Jazz Duets 2 Trombs/Rhythm Section
MMO CD 3901	Easy Solos: Student Level, v. I
MMO CD 3902	Easy Solos: Student Level, v. II
MMO CD 3920	Teacher's Partner: Basic Studies
MMO CD 7010	Twelve Classic Jazz Standards
MMO CD 7011	Twelve More Classic Jazz Standards
MMO CD 3931	World Favorites: 41 Easy Selections

And enjoy these fine accompaniment editions from other select publishers, including Hal Leonard, Alfred Publications, Music Sales, Jamey Aebersold and others!

MMO CD3936AP	Gordon Goodwin's Big Phat Band Play-Along Series
MMO CD3937AP	Harry Potter and the Goblet of Fire
MMO CD3938AP	Star Wars Trilogy 1,2,3
MMO CD3939AP	Lord of the Rings
MMO CD3940AP	Harry Potter and the Chamber of Secrets
MMO CD3942AP	Patriotic Instrumental Solos
MMO CD3944AP	Christmas Instrumental Solos: Carols/Traditions
MMO CD3945AP	James Bond 007 Collection
MMO DVD3946MS	A New Tune A Day for (CD/DVD
MMO CD3947HL	Ballads - 12 Play-Along Solos w/piano
MMO CD3948HL	Beginning Trombone Solos/Canadian Brass
MMO CD3949HL	Master Solos: Intermediate Level
MMO CD3950HL	Hymns for the Master
MMO CD3951HL	Easy Trombone Solos
MMO CD3952HL	Favorite Movie Themes
MMO CD3953HL	Essential Elements For Jazz Ensemble
MMO CD3954HL	Easy Disney Favorites
MMO CD3955HL	Intermediate Trombone Solos - Canadian Brass
MMO CD3956AP	Great Movie Instrumental Solos (Levels 2-3)
MMO CD3957HL	Andrew Lloyd Webber Classics minus Trombone
MMO CD3958AP	Alfred Solotracks: Dixieland
MMO CD3959HL	Album for Trombone and Piano, vol.I (very easy) (Dowani)
MMO CD3960HL	Album for Trombone and Piano, vol.II (easy) (Dowani)
MMO CD3961HL	Album for Trombone and Piano, vol.III (easy) (Dowani)
MMO CD3962HL	Top of the Charts
MMO CD3963AP	The Music of Bill Watrous
MMO CD3964HL	Big Band Play-Along, vol. 01: Swing Favorites
MMO CD3965HL	Jazz Trombone Tunes: Level/Grade 1
MMO CD3966HL	Jazz Trombone Tunes: Level/Grade 2
MMO CD3967HL	Jazz Trombone Tunes: Level/Grade 3
MMO CD3968CF	Trombonisms
MMO CD3969HL	Play Mozart-Trombone
MMO CD3970HL	World Famous Folksongs
MMO CD3971HL	Big Band Play-Along, vol. 02: Popular Hits
MMO CD3978AP	Jazz & Blues Playalong Solos For Trombone
MMO CD3979HL	Lennon and McCartney Solos For Trombone
MMO CD3981HL	Praise Songs: Instrumental Play-Along Pack
MMO CD3982HL	Big Band Play-Along, vol. 04: Jazz Classics
MMO CD3983AP	Rolling Stones: 12 Selections from the 500 Greatest Songs of All Time
MMO CD3984AP	Indiana Jones & the Kingdom of the Crystal Skull (Selections)
MMO CD3986HL	Big Band Play-Along, vol. 05: Christmas Favorites
MMO CD3987HL	Movie Themes
MMO CD3989HL	Baching Around the Christmas Tree
MMO CD3990HL	Instrumental Play-Along: Les Miserables
MMO CD3991CF	Arban's Famous Method for Trombone (Platinum Edition)
MMO CD3992AP	Easy Rock Instrumental Solos Level 1
MMO CD3993AP	Harry Potter (Selections): Level 2-3
MMO CD3994AP	Easy Popular Movie Instrumental Solos w/Piano Accompaniment - Level 1
MMO CD3995HL	Soul Hits-Trombone
MMO CD5841HL	Jazz Duets & Solos Play Along: Steven Mead
MMO CD5901HL	Instrumental Play-Along: A New Musical - Wicked
MMO CD5902HL	Instrumental Play-Along: High School Musical 2
MMO CD5903AP	The Wizard of Oz Instrumental Solos
MMO CD5904AP	Easy Christmas Instrumental Solos
MMO CD5905AP	Instrumental Solos by Special Arrangement

MMO CD5906HL	Instrumental Play-Along: Best of Metallica
MMO CD5907HL	Instrumental Play-Along: Elvis Presley
MMO CD5908HL	Instrumental Play-Along: Best of Bach
MMO CD5909AP	Christmas Instrumental Solos w/Piano accomp.
MMO CD5910AP	Classic Movie Instrumental Solos
MMO MB5911CF	Ear Training for Trombone by David Vining (Book Only)
MMO CD5912TP	Contest & Festival Performances Pieces/ Various Composers
MMO MB5913CF	Protocol: Guide to Collegiate Audition Process (Book Only)
MMO MB5914CF	Arthur Pryor Solos for Trombone (Book Only)
MMO MB5915CF	14 Duets for Trombone (Book Only)
MMO CD5916JA	How to Play Lead Trombone in a Big Band
MMO CD5917HL	Essential Elements 2000 Plus DVD: Comprehensive Band Method (Book/CD + DVD)
MMO CD5918HL	Rubank Concert and Contest Collections
MMO CD5919AP	Classic Rock Instrumental Solos
MMO CD5921HL	Big Band Play-Along, vol. 06: Latin
MMO CD5922HL	Big Band Play-Along, vol. 07: Standards
MMO CD5923HL	Super Solos: Trombone
MMO CD5924HL	Acoustic Rock: Trombone
MMO CD5925HL	Michael Jackson Instrumental Solos
MMO CD5926HL	Skillful Duets: Trombone/Euphonium BC
MMO CD5928HL	Nova Bossa
MMO CD5930HL	Moments of Swing
MMO CD5931HL	Swing To Me
MMO CD5932HL	Play Klezmer!
MMO CD5933HL	Missa Brevis for Trombone and Organ
MMO CD5934HL	The Easy Sound of Pop, Rock & Blues
MMO CD5935HL	Play Bach: 8 Famous Works for Trombone/Euphonium
MMO CD5936HL	Play Handel
MMO CD5937SAN	Hip To The Blues - Jazz Duets
MMO CD5939SAN	Exceptional Classics
MMO CD5940SAN	Promises Wedding Classics
MMO CD5941SAN	101 Popular Songs
MMO CD5942SAN	Inspirational Hymns
MMO CD5943SAN	Essential Standards
MMO CD5944SAN	Latin Favorites
MMO CD5945SAN	Know Before You Blow - Jazz Modes
MMO CD5946SAN	Know Before You Blow - Blues
MMO CD5947SAN	Classical Duets
MMO CD5948HL	Worship Favorites: Instrumental Play-Along for Trombone
MMO CD5949CF	Repertoire Classics for Trombone (Book/MP3 Data CD)
MMO CD5950CF	Melodious Etudes for Trombone (Book/MP3 Data CD)
MMO CD5951HL	Solos for the Trombone Player
MMO CD7040IR	Instrumental Resources: Trombone, Disc 1 – Daily Routines
MMO CD7901HL	Latin Themes for Trombone
MMO CD7902HL	Big Band Play-Along, vol. 03: Duke Ellington
MMO CD7903CF	Contest & Festival Performance Solos for Trombone
MMO CD7904HL	Irving Berlin's God Bless America & Other Star-Spangled Songs
MMO CD7905CF	Playing with the Band: March Melodies
MMO CD7906CF	Playing with the Band: At Christmas
MMO CD7907HL	Instrumental Play-Along: High School Musical 3: Trombone
MMO CD7908HL	Tchaikovsky's The Nutcracker-Trombone
MMO CD7909AP	Sittin' In with the Big Band-Jazz Ensemble Play-Along
MMO CD7910HL	Fiesta: Mexican and South American Favorites
MMO CD7911HL	Classic Praise
MMO CD7912CF	Händel: The Harmonious Blacksmith
MMO CD7913CF	Vivaldi: Largo and Allegro
MMO CD7914CF	Pryor: Fantastic Polka
MMO CD7915CF	Pryor: Thoughts of Love
MMO CD7916HL	Jazz Rock in the USA/Trombone
MMO CD7917HL	Jazz Rock And R&B/Trombone
MMO CD7918HL	Jazz Tracks Trombone Bc/Tc
MMO CD7919HL	All Jazz Book/CD Tromb Bc/Tc 11 Pieces In Swinging Styles
MMO CD7920HL	Jiggs Whigham Play Along Jazz Solos/Trombone

MMO CD7921HL	Jazzmatazz
MMO CD7922HL	Play 'Em Right Jazz, vol. 2
MMO CD7923HL	Play 'Em Right Jazz, vol. 1
MMO CD7925CF	Schumann: Träumerei (from 'Scenes from Childhood')
MMO CD7926CF	Easy Hymn Favorites w/Piano Accompaniment: Trombone
MMO CD7927HL	Irish Favorites: Trombone
MMO CD7928NM	"Bugs" Bower's Play With a Pro - Trombone
MMO CD7929HL	Instrumental Play-Along: Classic Rock Trombone
MMO CD7930HL	Peanuts™ (Vince Guaraldi) minus Trombone
MMO CD7931HL	Twilight - New Moon minus Trombone
MMO CD7932AP	Favorite Hymns Instrumental Solos
MMO CD7937CF	18 Intermediate Christmas Favorites (Book + Data/Accomp.CD)
MMO CD7938HL	Instrumental Play Along: Glee
MMO CD7939HL	Best of Beethoven
MMO CD7940HL	Christmas Favorites
MMO CD7941HL	Christmas Carols
MMO CD7942AP	World of Warcraft Instrumental Solos
MMO CD7943CF	I used to play Trombone by Larry Clark (Book/mp3 CD w/piano score pdf)
MMO CD7944HL	Berklee Practice Method: Trombone
MMO CD7945	Henry Mancini: Trombone
MMO CD7947HL	Feeling Good Trombone Easy Intermed. w/Piano Accompaniment
MMO CD7948HL	Easy Swing Pop Trombone - Play-Along
MMO CD7949HL	Bigger Swop For Trombone/Euphonium Basso Continuo/Treble Clef
MMO CD7950HL	Studies in Rhythm Trombone
MMO CD7951HL	Rhapsody 2 Solo Pieces w/Wind Ensemble Accompaniment Trombone Play-Along
MMO CD7952HL	Blues & Greens Trombone (Intermed.) Intl Play-Along
MMO CD7953HL	Power of Pop Trombone Book Easy level - Play-Along
MMO CD7954HL	The Swinging Beginning Trombone- Play-Along
MMO CD7955HL	Swing Starters
MMO CD7956HL	Kids Play Solo
MMO CD7957HL	Let's Play Reggae, Blues, Pop, Rock & Dance Trombone
MMO CD7958HL	Rock Connections Trombone/Euphonium
MMO CD7959HL	My First Melodies 34 Children's Tines -Trombone
MMO CD7960HL	Kids Play Blues Trombone Book/CE
MMO CD7961HL	Trombone Romance Play-Along
MMO CD7962HL	Jiggs Whigham Fusion 5 Solos For Trombone
MMO CD7964HL	The Concert Band at Home
MMO CD7965HL	Play 'Em Right! Play-Along
MMO CD7967HL	Go Solo A Fun Collection of Original Pieces
MMO CD7968HL	More Swing Pop: Play w/a Real Band! Grade 3
MMO CD7978HL	The Sound of Pop, Rock, Blues, vol. 2 Play-Along
MMO CD7979HL	Play The Blues
MMO CD7980HL	Very Easy Swing Pop: Play w/A Real Band!
MMO CD7981CF	Forty Progressive Etudes for Trombone (Book/MP3 CD)
MMO CD7996	Santa's Little Helper Christmas Songbook (Includes CD)
MMO CD7997	Traditional Christmas Duets for Trombone (Includes CD)
MMO CD7999SAN	Patriotic Melodies: An American Songbook – Trombone
MMO CD8135CF	Corelli: Gigue
MMO CD8891AP	Pop & Rock Hits Instrumental Solos
MMO MB8986JA	Doodles - Trombone exercises (Book Only)
MMO CD9454AM	Jazz Conception by Jim Snidero for Bass Trombone
MMO CD11901LP	Creative Hymns for Trombone
MMO CD11902HL	Popular Hits
MMO CD11903AM	Brazilian and Afro-Cuban Jazz Conception
MMO CD11904AM	Easy Jazz Conception for Trombone
MMO CD11905AM	Intermediate Jazz Conception for Trombone
MMO CD11906AM	Jazz Conception by Jim Snidero for Trombone
MMO CD11907HL	Lennon & McCartney Favorites – Trombone
MMO CD11908AM	Playing Through the Blues
MMO CD11909HL	West Side Story
MMO CD11910HL	Instrumental Play-Along: Taylor Swift
MMO CD11911HL	Queen – Trombone
MMO MB11912	Sing It First: Wycliffe Gordon's Unique Approach to Trombone Playing (Book Only)
MMO CD11913	Motown Classics For Trombone

MMO CD11914	Disney Classics Instrumental Play-Along: Trombone
MMO CD11915	Favorite Classical Melodies Instrumental: Trombone
MMO CD11916	Harry Potter Instrumental Solos: Trombone
MMO CD11917	Instrumental Play-Along: Great Themes – Trombone
MMO CDR11918	Classical Solos: 15 Easy Trombone Solos for Contest and Performance (Book/CD-ROM)
MMO CD11919	Instrumental Play-Along: Fantasia 2000 – Trombone
MMO CD11920	Instrumental Play-Along – Celtic Melodies: Trombone
MMO CD11921	Berger: Contemporary Jazz Studies - Trombone, vol. 1
MMO CD11922	Berger: Contemporary Jazz Studies - Trombone, vol. 2
MMO CD11923	Berger: Contemporary Jazz Studies - Trombone, vol. 3
MMO CD11924	Berger: Contemporary Jazz Studies - Trombone, vol. 4
MMO CD11925	Reading Key Jazz Rhythms for Trombone
MMO CD11926	14 Advanced Christmas Favorites Trombone (Book/MP3 CD)
MMO CD11927	Jazz Phrasing for Trombone, vol.1 (2 CD set)
MMO CDR11928	Alfred Ultimate Movie Instrumental Solos (Book/MP3 CD)

MMO MB11929	Chops for Trombone by Frank T. Williams (book only)
MMO MB11930	Chops: Trombone (Book Only)
MMO CD11931HL	Today's Women of Pop
MMO CD11932	Instrumental Play-Along: Stephen Sondheim Broadway Solos
MMO CD11933	Instrumental Play-Along – Broadway Hits for Trombone
MMO CD11934	Jazz Trombone CD Level/Grade 4 (Accomp CD/No Book)
MMO CD11935	Jazz Trombone CD Level/Grade 5 (Accomp CD/No Book)
MMO CD11936	Ultimate Pop & Rock Instrumental Solos – Trombone
MMO CD11937	Instrumental Play-Along: Folksongs - Trombone
MMOCD12248AM	Modern Jazz Classics, vol. 2: The Jazz Workshop Series, vol. 8
MMO CD23118HL	Play the Duke
MMO CD23119HL	Mambo No.5, Maria Maria and Other Latin Hits
MMO CD23120HL	Cool Yule
MMO CD23121HL	The Sound of Music
MMO CD23122HL	R&B Classics

Music Minus One

50 Executive Boulevard • Elmsford, New York 10523-1325

800-669-7464 (US) • 914-592-1188 (International) • e-mail: info@musicminusone.com

www.musicminusone.com

MMO 3936

ISBN 978-0-98967051-7